CONTENTS

4A

Where Are You From?

Mini Talk Look and listen. ▶ 🎧 03

Hi, I'm Junho. What's your name?

Hi, Junho. My name is Emma.

I'm from Korea. Where are you from?

I'm from France.

CHECK 04

1 What is the boy's name? a ☐ b ☐

2 Where is the girl from? a ☐ b ☐

Practice

A Listen and write the letter. 🎧 05   **B** Listen and repeat. 🎧 06

Where is she from?	Where is he from?
She's from France.	He's from Korea.

1 France ☐

2 Korea ☐

3 Canada ☐

4 China ☐

5 the U.S. ☐

6 Vietnam ☐

7 Australia ☐

8 Mexico ☐

Listen & Talk

(A) Listen and match. 🎧07

1

2

3

4

5

a Vietnam

b Mexico

c France

d the U.S.

e Australia

YOUR TURN
(B) Check and say.

Where are you from?

I'm from _____.

Korea

Canada

France

Write & Talk

Ⓐ Write, listen, and read. 🎧 08

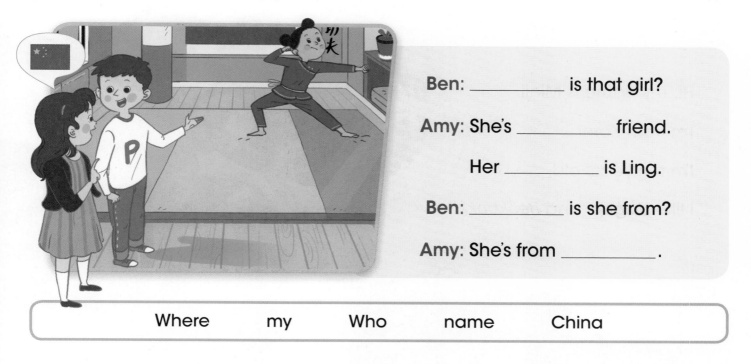

Ben: _____ is that girl?

Amy: She's _____ friend.

Her _____ is Ling.

Ben: _____ is she from?

Amy: She's from _____ .

| Where | my | Who | name | China |

Ⓑ Choose and write. Then ask and answer.

> Where is he/she from?

1

China

the U.S.

He's from _____

2

Vietnam

France

She's _____ .

3

Korea

Australia

_____

4

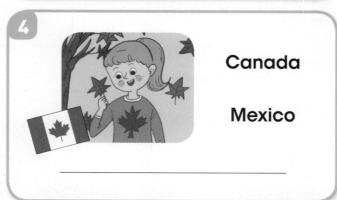

Canada

Mexico

_____

Reading

A Listen and read.

Hi, my name is Minji.

I'm from Korea.

I'm ten years old.

I like *bulgogi* and *tteokbokki*!

This is my friend, Antonio.

He's from Mexico.

He's eleven years old.

He likes tacos and burritos.

B Circle or write.

1   Minji is ten years old.   (T / F)

2   Antonio doesn't like burritos.   (T / F)

3   Where is Antonio from? ⋯▸ He's from _____ .

A Listen and repeat. 🎧 10

I – my   you – your
he – his   she – her

- He is from France. His name is Leo.
- She is from China. Her name is Mei.

B Circle and write.

1

This is _____ teddy bear. (I / my)

_____ love it. (I / My)

2

_____ name is Brian. (His / Her)

_____ is from Canada. (He / His)

3

_____ have a sister. (I / My)

_____ name is Grace. (His / Her)

4

Is that _____ brother? (you / your)

_____ is cool. (He / His)

5

_____ name is Bian. (Her / She)

_____ is from Vietnam. (Her / She)

Check-Up

Ⓐ Listen and choose. 🎧11

1 ⓐ ⓑ

2 ⓐ ⓑ

3 ⓐ ⓑ

4 ⓐ ⓑ

Ⓑ Listen and match. 🎧12

1 2 3 4

the U.S.   France   Vietnam   Canada

Ⓒ Listen and choose. 🎧13

1  ⓐ She's from Mexico.

ⓑ She's from Australia.

Mary

2  ⓐ He's from Korea.

ⓑ He's from China.

Chen

D Look and write.

1

A: Where are you from?

B: I'm _____ _____.

2

A: Where is he from?

B: He's _____ _____.

3

_____ is from _____.

_____ name is Bella.

E Write and say.

1

A: Where is he from?

B: _____

2

A: Where is she from?

B: _____

Do You Like Watching Movies?

Mini Talk Look and listen. ▶ 🎧16

Do you like watching movies?

Yes, I do.

How about this movie?

It looks fun.
Let's watch the movie!

Aaaaah!

CHECK 17

1 Where are the girl and the boy? ⓐ ☐ ⓑ ☐
2 Does the boy like watching movies? ⓐ ☐ ⓑ ☐

Practice

A Listen and write the letter. 18 **B** Listen and repeat. 19

Do you like **fishing**? | Yes, I do. | No, I don't.

fishing ☐

flying drones ☐

watching movies ☐

taking pictures ☐

playing computer games ☐

riding a bike ☐

listening to music ☐

Listen & Talk

A Listen, number, and circle. 🎧 20

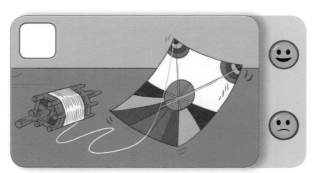

YOUR TURN

B Check and say.

Do you like _____?

Yes, I do. / No, I don't.

listening to music

flying drones

riding a bike

Write & Talk

A Write, listen, and read. 🎧21

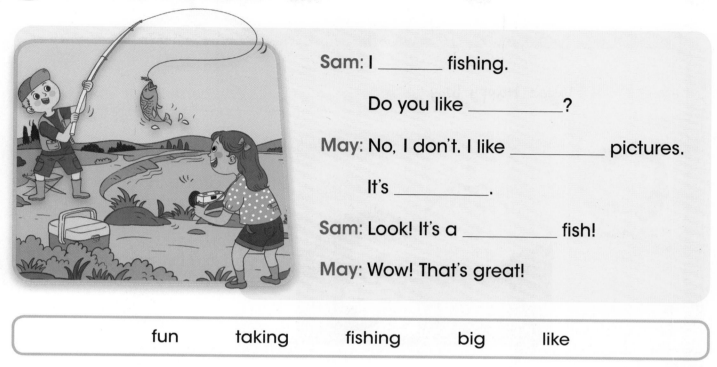

Sam: I _____ fishing.

Do you like _____?

May: No, I don't. I like _____ pictures.

It's _____.

Sam: Look! It's a _____ fish!

May: Wow! That's great!

| fun | taking | fishing | big | like |

B Match and write. Then ask and answer.

1 playing 🙂

2 singing 🙂

3 watching 🙁

movies   computer games   songs

1 A: Do you like _____?   B: Yes, I _____.

2 A: Do you _____?   B: _____

3 A: Do _____?   B: _____

Reading

A Listen and read. 🎧22

Maya's Happy Blog

Maya

I like flying drones.

I fly my drone in the park.

It's very exciting.

Do you like flying drones?

Hello!

Kevin
No, I don't. I can't fly drones.

I like listening to music. I like hip-hop music.

It's very cool.

Maya
I like hip-hop music, too.

B Circle or write.

1 Maya likes flying kites.   (T / F)

2 Kevin can't fly drones.   (T / F)

3 Kevin likes _____ to _____.

Build Up

A Listen and repeat. 23

like playing

I play computer games. ···▸ I like playing computer games.

She takes pictures. ···▸ She likes taking pictures.

B Look and write.

1

I like _____ movies.

watching

flying

dancing

riding

listening

2

We like _____ to music.

3

My friend and I like _____ kites.

4

He likes _____ a bike.

5

She likes singing and _____.

Check-Up

A Listen and number. 24

B Listen and choose. 25

1  ⓐ ⓑ

2  ⓐ ⓑ

3  ⓐ ⓑ

4  ⓐ ⓑ

C Listen and choose. 26

1 Jane likes _____.

  ⓐ dancing   ⓑ singing songs   ⓒ listening to music

2 Steve likes _____.

  ⓐ fishing   ⓑ flying kites   ⓒ riding a bike

D Write and match.

1  2  3  4

1 | Do you like _____? | •   • | Yes, she does. |

2 | Do you _____? | •   • | Yes, I do. It's fun. |

3 | Does he like _____? | •   • | No, I don't. |

4 | Does she _____? | •   • | No, he doesn't. |

E Write and say.

1

A: _____

B: Yes, I do. It's fun.

2

A: _____

B: No, I don't.

Ⓐ Read and write.

| I'm from Mexico. | Do you like flying drones? | Where are you from? |

B Look and write.

1  2  3

1 A: Where are you from?   B: I'm from _____.

2 A: Where is he from?   B: He's _____.

3 A: Where is she from?   B: She's _____.

France

Canada

Vietnam

C Match and check.

1    Do you like •   • riding a bike?

☐ Yes, he does. ☐ No, he doesn't.

2    Does she like •   • taking pictures?

☐ Yes, she does. ☐ No, she doesn't.

3    Does he like •   • listening to music?

☐ Yes, I do. ☐ No, I don't.

Let's Go Shopping Tomorrow

Mini Talk Look and listen.

Hello?

Hi, Tim.

Hi, Kate. This is Tim.

Sounds good. I need new socks.

Let's go shopping tomorrow.

CHECK 30

1 What does Tim say? a ☐ b ☐

2 What does Kate need? a ☐ b ☐

Practice

A Listen and write the letter. 🎧31   **B** Listen and repeat. 🎧32

Let's **go camping**.

Sounds good.

Sorry, I can't. I'm busy.

1 go camping
2 go hiking
3 go skiing
4 go skating
5 go jogging
6 go in-line skating
7 go swimming
8 go shopping

Listen & Talk

A Listen, number, and circle. 🎧 33

Let's _____ tomorrow.

Sounds good. / Sorry, I can't.

YOUR TURN
B Check and say.

go in-line skating

go skiing

go hiking

Write & Talk

A Write, listen, and read. 🎧 34

Ann: Hello, Sue. _____ is Ann.

Let's go _____ this afternoon.

Sue: _____, I can't.

I have a _____ class.

Ann: How about _____?

Sue: Okay. See you tomorrow.

tomorrow	piano	swimming	This	Sorry

B Follow and write. Then ask and answer.

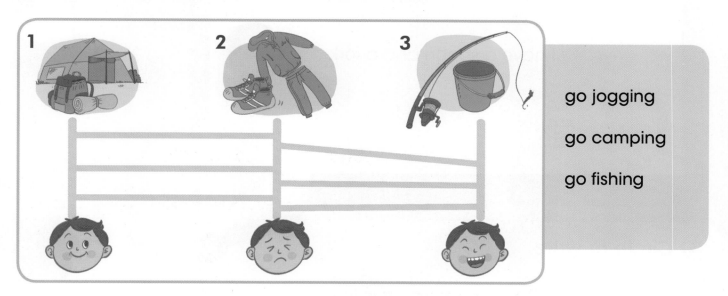

go jogging

go camping

go fishing

1 A: Let's _____.   B: Sounds good.

2 A: Let's _____.   B: _____, I can't.

3 A: Let's _____.   B: _____ great.

Reading

Listen and read. 35

Ken: Let's go camping this weekend.

Ted: That's a good idea.
I like camping.
I like eating steak, too.

Do you have a tent?

Ken: Yes, I do.
I have camping chairs, too.
What do you have?

Ted: I have a spoon and a fork.

Ken: ...

B **Circle or write.**

1 Ted (can / can't) go camping this weekend.

2 Ted likes (eating steak / eating fish).

3 Ken has a _____ and _____ .

Build Up

A Listen and repeat.

 Let's go skating.

go skating

 Let's go camping.

B Look and write.

| hiking | swimming | jogging | skiing | in-line skating |

1 Let's go _____ tomorrow.

2 It's sunny.

Let's _____ _____ today.

3 It's hot today.

Let's _____ _____ this afternoon.

4 It's snowing.

_____ _____ _____ today.

5 _____ _____ _____ this weekend.

Check-Up

A Listen and match. 37

1   2   3   4

a    b    c    d

B Listen and number. 38

C Listen and circle. 39

 1 Kevin (can / can't) go swimming this weekend.

2 Sally (can / can't) go hiking today.

D Look and write.

1

A: Let's _____ _____.

B: _____ good.

2

A: Let's _____ _____.

B: Sorry, I _____. I'm busy.

3

A: Let's _____ _____ tomorrow.

B: That's a _____ _____.

E Write and say.

1

A: _____

B: Sounds good.

2

A: _____

B: Sorry, I can't. I'm tired.

What Do You Do After School?

What do you do after school, Amy?

I ride my bike. What about you, John?

I help my dad.

Wow! You're a good boy.

1 What does Amy do after school? a ☐ b ☐
2 What does John do after school? a ☐ b ☐

Practice

A Listen and write the letter. 🎧 44   **B** Listen and repeat. 🎧 45

| What do you do after school? | I play tennis. |

1

play tennis ☐

2

play with friends ☐

3

help my mom ☐

4

walk my dog ☐

5

do my homework ☐

6

take an English class ☐

7

take a robot class ☐

8

have a piano lesson ☐

Listen & Talk

A Listen and circle T or F. 🎧 46

1

T
F

2

T
F

3

T
F

4

T
F

5

T
F

6

T
F

YOUR TURN

B Check and say.

What do you do after school?

I _____.

play with friends

take an English class

play tennis

Write & Talk

A Write, listen, and read. 🎧47

Nora: What do you do _____?

Ken: I _____ with friends.

What about you?

Nora: I take a _____ class.

I _____ a robot on Mondays.

Ken: Sounds fun.

| play soccer | robot | after school | make |

B Look and write. Then ask and answer.

> What does he/she do after dinner?

Matt's room Emily's room Joey's room

1   He _____.

2   She _____.

3   He _____.

| watches TV |
| reads books |
| has a piano lesson |

Reading

A Listen and read.  🎧 48

Happy Classroom News

New Friend

David Baker

"I help my mom after school."

What do you do after school?

I take an English class.
I watch music videos.
I help my mom.

What about your sister, Kate?

Kate walks her dog after school.
She plays with her dog.
Then she watches TV.

B Circle or choose.

1 David takes (a math class / an English class) after school.

2 David helps (his mom / his dad) after school.

3 Kate _____ after school.

    ⓐ watches music videos   **ⓑ** walks her dog   **ⓒ** plays with friends

Build Up

A Listen and repeat. 🎧49

-s / -es

read – reads	do – does	
play – plays	watch – watches	
take – takes	wash – washes	

- I read books.
- He plays baseball.
- She watches a movie.

B Choose, change, and write.

1

He ___takes___ a cooking class.

2

She _____ TV at home.

3

Ted _____ many books.

4

Julie _____ her hands.

5

Tom _____ his homework.

read
wash
take
do
watch

Check-Up

A Listen and number.

B Listen and choose.

1  ⓐ ⓑ ⓒ

2  ⓐ ⓑ ⓒ

3  ⓐ ⓑ ⓒ

4  ⓐ ⓑ ⓒ

C Listen and circle T or F.

1 Betty takes an English class after school. (T / F)

2 Henry walks his dog every day. (T / F)

D Look and write.

1

A: _____ do you do after school?

B: I _____ my _____.

2

A: What _____ he do after school?

B: He _____ his _____.

3

A: I _____ books after school.
What about you?

B: I _____ music videos.

E Write and say.

1

A: What do you do after school?

B: _____

2

A: What do you do after school?

B: _____

Review 2

(A) Read and write.

Let's go in-line skating.	I go swimming with my dad.
Sorry, I can't.	What do you do after school?

I have a piano lesson.

What about you?

Dad, let's go swimming.

Sounds good.

B Match and write the number.

1 | What do you do after school? | • | • | He plays with friends.

2 | What does she do after dinner? | • | • | She walks her dog.

3 | What does he do after school? | • | • | I do my homework.

C Unscramble and check.

1

A: _____ this afternoon.
(shopping / go / Let's)

B: ☐ Okay.　　☐ Sorry, I can't.

2

A: _____ tomorrow.
(go / Let's / in-line skating)

B: ☐ Sounds good.　　☐ Sorry, I can't.

3

A: _____ this weekend.
(Let's / hiking / go)

B: ☐ Sounds good.　　☐ Sorry, I can't.

Mini Talk Look and listen. ▶ 55

What time do you get up?

I get up at 6:30.

That's very early.

I go jogging every morning.

That's great!

○ CHECK 56

1 What time does the boy get up? a ☐ b ☐
2 What does the boy do every morning? a ☐ b ☐

Practice

A Listen and write the letter. 🎧57   **B** Listen and repeat. 🎧58

| What time do you get up? | I get up at 7:30. |

get up ☐

have breakfast ☐

go to bed ☐

have dinner ☐

exercise ☐

go to school ☐

have lunch ☐

go home ☐

Listen & Talk

A Listen and match. 59

1 •  •

2 •  •

3 •  •

4 •  •

5 •  •

YOUR TURN
B Draw and say.

What time do you go to school?

I go to school at _____ : _____.

Write & Talk

A Write, listen, and read. 🎧60

Ron: _____ do you go home?

Lisa: I _____ at 6 o'clock.

Ron: That's very late.

   What do you do _____ school?

Lisa: I go in-line skating every day.

   And I have a _____ today.

Ron: Wow, you are very _____.

| dance class | after | What time | go home | busy |

B Look and write. Then ask and answer.

What time do you ~?

1 I _____ at 7:00.

2 I _____ at 12:30.

3 I _____ at 10:30.

get up
go to bed
have lunch

Reading

(A) Listen and read. 🎧 61

Max lives in space.

He gets up at 7 o'clock.

He has breakfast at 7:30.

He exercises at 9 o'clock.

He rides a bike every day.

He listens to music in the afternoon.

He reads books, too.

He has dinner at 6:30.

He goes to bed at 10 o'clock.

(B) Circle or write.

1 Max gets up at 7 o'clock.   (T / F)

2 Max rides a bike in the afternoon. (T / F)

3 Max _____ at 10 o'clock.

Build Up

(A) Listen and repeat. 🎧62

-es / -ies / has

watch – watch**es**	wash – wash**es**	• I watch TV. He watch**es** a movie.
go – go**es**	do – do**es**	• I study English. He stud**ies** math.
study – stud**ies**	have – **has**	• I have lunch. She **has** dinner.

(B) Choose, change, and write.

watch TV	study science	go to school	do his homework	have lunch

1

He _____ after dinner.

2

She _____ at 8.

3

Tom _____ at 4:30.

4

My sister _____ after school.

5

My brother _____ at 12.

Check-Up

A Listen and check. 🎧 63

1

2

3

4

B Listen and number. Then circle. 🎧 64

| 5:00 |
| 7:00 |

| 9:20 |
| 10:20 |

| 5:10 |
| 6:10 |

| 8:40 |
| 9:40 |

C Listen and match. 🎧 65

1 Sally

2 Emma

• goes to bed •   • at 6:30.

• goes jogging •   • at 8:00.

• goes home •   • at 11:00.

D Look and write.

1

A: What time do you _____?

B: I _____ at 8:30.

2

A: What time do you _____?

B: I _____ at 10:50.

3

A: What time _____?

B: I _____ at 5 o'clock.

E Write and say.

1

A: What time do you get up?

B: _____

2

A: _____

B: I have dinner at 6:30.

I Have Some Snacks in My Bag

Mini Talk Look and listen. ▶ 🎧68

Do you have a blanket, Tom?

What do you have, Alex?

Yes, I have a blanket in my bag.

I have some snacks.
I have comic books, too.

CHECK 🎧69

1 What does Tom have?   a ☐ b ☐
2 Does Alex have snacks?   a ☐ b ☐

46

Practice

A Listen and write the letter. 🎧 70   **B** Listen and repeat. 🎧 71

| What does she have? | What does he have? |
| She has a **blanket**. | He has a **map**. |

1 blanket ⬜

2 map ⬜

3 water bottle ⬜

4 pot ⬜

5 camera ⬜

6 flashlight ⬜

7 lunchbox ⬜

8 sleeping bag ⬜

Listen & Talk

A Listen and write the letter. 🎧 72

1 2 3

4 5 6

ⓐ ⓑ ⓒ ⓓ ⓔ ⓕ

What do you have in your bag?

I have a _____ .

B YOUR TURN Check and say.

map

sleeping bag

tent

48

Write & Talk

A Write, listen, and read. 🎧 73

Pete: I'm thirsty. Do you _____ some water?

Sally: No, I don't. Eva has a _____.

Pete: _____ she have a cup, too?

Sally: I don't _____.

Look. Kevin has a _____.

Pete: Oh, good.

| cup | have | Does | know | water bottle |

B Follow and write. Then ask and answer.

What does he/she have?

map

blanket

sleeping bag

water bottle

1 She has a _____.

2 He _____.

3 _____

4 _____

Reading

 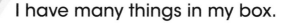
I have many things in my box.

I have my teddy bear. It's old.

I have a camera and an old map.

I have my pictures, too.

This is my brother's toy box.

What does Tom have?

He has a car.

He has a kite and a robot.

Eek! He has a frog!

B Circle or write.

1 Tina has a camera in her box.   (T / F)

2 Tina doesn't have books in her box.   (T / F)

3 What does Tom have in his box?

····> He has _____, a kite, a robot, and _____.

Build Up

A Listen and repeat. 🎧 75

has, doesn't have

| ⃝ 📷 I **have** a camera. | ⃝ 🗺 He **has** a map. |
| ✕ 🗺 I **don't have** a map. | ✕ 📷 He **doesn't have** a camera. |

B Look and write.

1

I _____ a blanket.

I _____ a tent.

2

Kate _____ a flashlight.

She _____ a pot.

3

We _____ sleeping bags.

We _____ a tent.

4

Alex _____ a car.

He _____ a bike.

5

The man _____ pigs.

He _____ cows.

A Listen and number. 🎧76

B Listen and match. 🎧77

1

2

3

4

a

b

c

d

C Listen and circle. 🎧78

1   Paul has (a pot / a map) in his bag.

2   Lily has (a water bottle / a flashlight).

D Look and write.

1

A: What does Mark have?

B: He _____ a _____.

2

I _____ a pot.

I _____ a cup.

3

He _____ a tent.

He _____ a sleeping bag.

E Write and say.

1

A: What does he have?

B: _____

2

A: _____

B: She has a camera.

Ⓐ Read and write.

What time do you exercise?   I have some snacks in my bag.
I get up at 7:30.

B Look and write.

1

A: What time do you have breakfast?

B: I _____ at _____.

2

A: _____ do you go to school?

B: I _____ at 8 o'clock.

3

A: _____ do you _____?

B: I go home at 3:30.

C Check or circle.

1

A: What do you have?

B: ☐ I have a blanket.　　☐ I have a tent.

2

A: What does she have?

B: ☐ She has a map.　　☐ She has a lunchbox.

3

He (has / doesn't have) a water bottle.

But he (has / doesn't have) a cup.

Whose Ball Is This?

Mini Talk Look and listen. ▶ 🎧 81

Ouch!!!

Jenny, is this your ball?

Whose ball is it?

No, it isn't. It's not mine.

It's Bob's.

Sorry, Dad. It's mine.

CHECK 82

1 What does the man have? a ☐ b ☐
2 Whose ball is it? a ☐ b ☐

Practice

A Listen and write the letter. 🎧 83   **B** Listen and repeat. 🎧 84

| Whose mirror is this? | It's Emily's. |

1 mirror ☐

2 paintbrush ☐

3 cell phone ☐

4 painting ☐

Linda

Kevin

Emily

Tom

Peter

Tina

Judy

David

5 toothbrush ☐

6 wallet ☐

7 textbook ☐

8 helmet ☐

ENGLISH
A B C D

Listen & Talk

(A) Listen and match. 🎧 85

1

2

3

4

5

YOUR TURN
(B) Check and say.

Whose _____ is this?

It's _____.

mirror

toothbrush

wallet

Write & Talk

A Write, listen, and read. 🎧 86

Billy: Look at this _____. It's cute.

Lucy: _____ helmet is this?

Billy: It's _____.

She likes ladybugs.

Lucy: Emily, is this _____?

Emily: Yes, it's _____. Thank you.

| Whose | helmet | mine | yours | Emily's helmet |

B Look and write. Then ask and answer.

1 Whose watch is this?

It's Dave's _____.

2 Whose cell phone is this?

It's _____.

3 Whose balloons are these?

They're _____.

4 Whose hairpins are these?

They're _____.

Reading

Ⓐ Listen and read. 🎧87

Whose dress is this?

It's pink. Anna likes pink.

"Is this Anna's dress?"

"Yes, it is."

Whose hat is that?

It's yellow. Dora likes yellow.

"Is that yours, Dora?

"Yes, it's mine."

The shoes are pretty.

They're red and white.

Whose shoes are these?

They're Cindy's.

Ⓑ Circle or choose.

1   Anna's (dress / hat) is pink.

2   The yellow (shoe / hat) is (Dora's / Cindy's).

3   Whose shoes are they?

ⓐ They're Dora's.   ⓑ They're Anna's.   ⓒ They're Cindy's.

Build Up

Ⓐ Listen and repeat. 🎧88

mine	yours	hers	his

my watch ⋯▸ mine

your scarf ⋯▸ yours

Jane's cap ⋯▸ her cap ⋯▸ hers

Tom's bag ⋯▸ his bag ⋯▸ his

Ⓑ Write or circle. Then match.

1 This is my bike.

⋯▸ This is _____.

2 Is this your cell phone?

⋯▸ Is this _____?

3 Is that Linda's umbrella?

⋯▸ Is that (his / her) umbrella?

⋯▸ Is that _____?

4 Is this Mike's toothbrush?

⋯▸ Is this (his / her) toothbrush?

⋯▸ Is this _____?

Check-Up

A Listen and match. 🎧89

1   2   3   4

B Listen and choose. 🎧90

1  ⓐ ⓑ

2  ⓐ ⓑ

3  ⓐ ⓑ

4  ⓐ ⓑ

C Listen and circle. 🎧91

1  It's (Sara's / Sally's) (paintbrush / hairpin).

2  It's (Leo's / Nick's) (helmet / umbrella).

D Unscramble and circle.

1

A: _____?
(is / Whose / that / mirror)

B: It's (Kate / Kate's).

2

A: _____?
(this / textbook / Whose / is)

Is it yours?

B: No, it's not (yours / mine). It's Fred's.

3

A: _____?
(Whose / is / wallet / this)

Is it Lucy's?

B: Yes, it's (her / hers).

E Write and say.

1

A: Whose paintbrush is that?

B: _____

2

A: _____

B: It's mine.

Where Is the Bookstore?

Mini Talk Look and listen. ▶ 🎧94

Excuse me.
Where is the bookstore?

It's next to the toy shop.

Toy shop?
Thank you.

You're welcome.

CHECK 🎧95

1 What does the boy ask? ⓐ ☐ ⓑ ☐
2 Where is the bookstore? ⓐ ☐ ⓑ ☐

Practice

Ⓐ Listen and write the letter. 🎧96

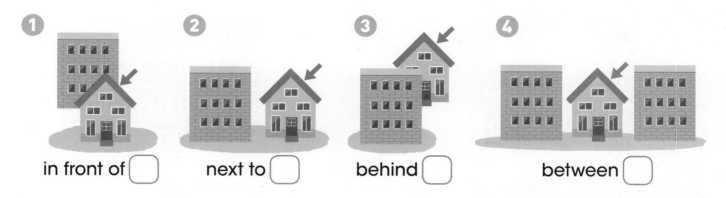

1	**2**	**3**	**4**
in front of ⬜	next to ⬜	behind ⬜	between ⬜

Ⓑ Listen and repeat. 🎧97

> Where is the train station? | It's next to the zoo.

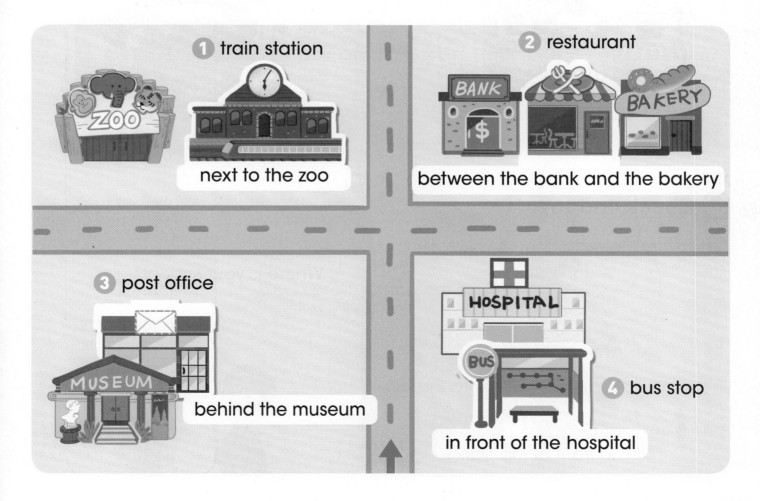

1 train station — next to the zoo

2 restaurant — between the bank and the bakery

3 post office — behind the museum

4 bus stop — in front of the hospital

Listen & Talk

Ⓐ Listen and write T or F. 🎧 98

1

2

3

4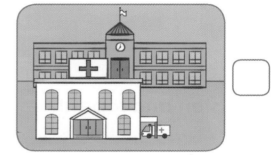

5

6

 **Ⓑ Check and say.**

behind the park

next to the park

in front of the park

Where is your school?

It's _____.

66

Write & Talk

(A) Write, listen, and read. 🎧 99

Eric: I'm _____. Let's eat _____.

Mary: Okay. Where is the _____?

Eric: It's over there. It's _____ the

bookstore _____ the post office.

Mary: Oh, I see it.

| pizza | restaurant | hungry | and | between |

Where is the ice cream shop?

(B) Look and write. Then ask and answer.

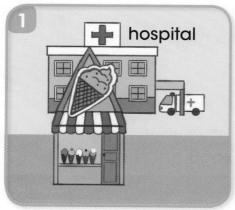

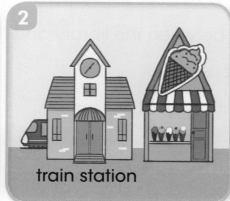

1 It's _____.

2 It's _____.

3 It's _____.

| next to |
| in front of |
| between … and … |

Reading

A Listen and read. 🎧 100

MY TOWN

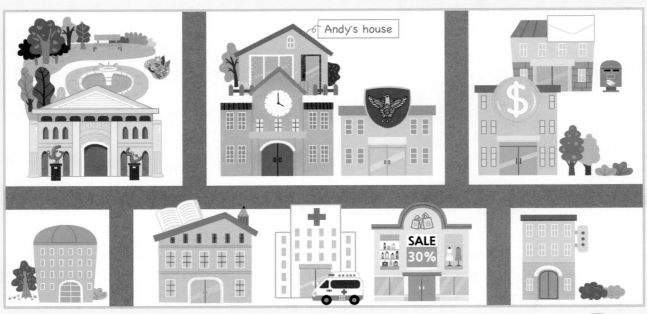

This is my town.

My school is next to the police station.

The museum is in front of the park.

The post office is behind the bank.

The hospital is between the library and the mall.

Where is my house?

It's over there. It's behind the school.

B Circle or write.

1   The park is behind the museum.   (T / F)

2   The library is between the mall and the hospital.   (T / F)

3   Where is Andy's house?

    ⋯➤ It's _____.

Build Up

A Listen and repeat. 🎧101

in front of   next to   behind   between

B Look and write.

1

The tree is _____ the house.

2
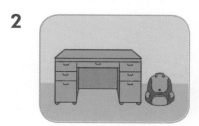

The school bag is _____ the desk.

3

The window is _____ the bookcase

_____ the closet.

4

The bike is _____ the bus stop.

5

The car is _____ the supermarket.

Check-Up

A Listen and write T or F. 🎧102

1

2

3

4

B Listen and choose. 🎧103

1  ⓐ ⓑ

2  ⓐ ⓑ

3  ⓐ ⓑ

4  ⓐ ⓑ

C Listen and write the letter. 🎧104

1 Where is the park? ☐

2 Where is the post office? ☐

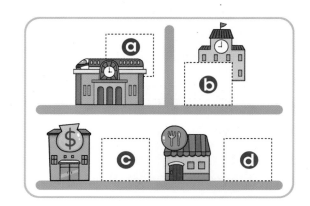

70

D Look and write.

1 A: Where is the _____? B: It's _____ the museum.

2 A: Where is the _____? B: It's _____ the bookstore.

3 A: Where is the _____? B: It's _____ the school and the hospital.

E Write and say.

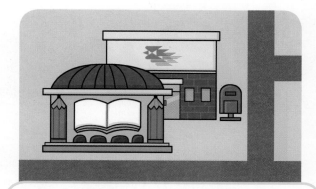

A: Where is the library?

B: _____

A: Where is the train station?

B: _____

Ⓐ Read and write.

Where is the bus stop?	Whose cell phone is this?
it's not mine	It's in front of the park

_____

Is it yours, Ann?

No, _____.

It's mine.

Let's go to the mall.

_____

It's next to the bank.

_____

_____, too.

Ⓑ Match and write.

1 It's _____ wallet. •

2 It's _____ mirror. •

3 It's _____ paintbrush. •

4 It's _____ painting. •

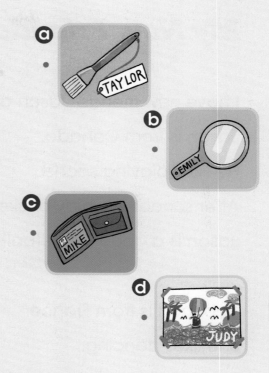

ⓐ TAYLOR

ⓑ EMILY

ⓒ MIKE

ⓓ JUDY

Ⓒ Look and write.

BOOKSTORE RESTAURANT BANK
SCHOOL
LIBRARY
POLICE STATION MUSEUM

between	next to	behind

1 A: Where is the museum?

   B: It's _____.

2 A: Where is the school?

   B: It's _____.

3 A: Where is the restaurant?

   B: It's _____

   _____.

My New Friends 🎧105

I have new friends, Jason and Rebecca.

Jason is from Canada.

He likes playing sports.

After school, we play basketball together.

Jason is a good basketball player.

Rebecca is from France.

She likes dancing.

Every Friday, we meet and dance together.

She is cool. She is a good dancer.

I like my new friends.

1 This story is about the boy's _____.

ⓐ new school   ⓑ new friends   ⓒ new teacher

2 Jason is from _____.

ⓐ France   ⓑ the U.S.   ⓒ Canada

3 Jason likes _____.

ⓐ dancing   ⓑ playing the piano   ⓒ playing sports

4 Rebecca is _____.

ⓐ Jason's sister

ⓑ a good dancer.

ⓒ a good basketball player

Writing Practice

What does Jason do after school? ⋯▸ He plays basketball.

1 What does Sally do after dinner?

⋯▸ She _____. (listen to music)

2 What does Mario do after school?

⋯▸ He _____. (take an English class)

Where Is Mr. Baker? 106

Kevin has lunch at the school cafeteria.

He finds a blue wallet there.

"Whose wallet is this?

Oh, here's the name Baker.

It's Mr. Baker's wallet."

Kevin goes to the music room.

It's next to the art room.

Kevin finds Mr. Baker.

"Hello, Mr. Baker. Is this your wallet?"

"Yes, it is. Thanks, Kevin."

1 This story is about _____.

    ⓐ finding a wallet   ⓑ finding Mr. Baker   ⓒ finding the art room

Comprehension

2 Kevin finds _____ at the school cafeteria.

    ⓐ a lunchbox   ⓑ Mr. Baker   ⓒ a blue wallet

3 Mr. Baker is in the _____.

    ⓐ cafeteria   ⓑ music room   ⓒ art room

4 The music room is _____ the art room.

    ⓐ behind   ⓑ next to   ⓒ in front of

Writing Practice

Whose wallet is this? ⋯▸ It's Mr. Baker's wallet.

1 Whose painting is it?

    ⋯▸ It's _____. (Paul)

2 Whose mirror is this?

    ⋯▸ It's _____. (Linda)

- **Present Simple**

verb + -s / -es / -ies					
bake	bakes		have	has	
bring	brings		help	helps	
buy	buys		make	makes	
catch	catches		meet	meets	
clean	cleans		paint	paints	
come	comes		play	plays	
cry	cries		read	reads	
dance	dances		ride	rides	
do	does		run	runs	
draw	draws		study	studies	
drink	drinks		take	takes	
eat	eats		teach	teaches	
finish	finishes		walk	walks	
fly	flies		wash	washes	
go	goes		watch	watches	

• -ing Forms

verb + -ing					
catch	catching		read	reading	
clean	cleaning		run	running	
come	coming		shop	shopping	
dance	dancing		sing	singing	
do	doing		skate	skating	
drive	driving		ski	skiing	
eat	eating		study	studying	
go	going		swim	swimming	
help	helping		take	taking	
jog	jogging		use	using	
jump	jumping		visit	visiting	
listen	listening		walk	walking	
make	making		wash	washing	
paint	painting		watch	watching	
play	playing		write	writing	

Word List 4A

Unit 1 Where Are You From?

Australia _____

Canada _____

China _____

France _____

her _____

his _____

Korea _____

Mexico _____

my _____

the U.S. _____

Vietnam _____

where _____

your _____

Unit 2 Do You Like Watching Movies?

dancing _____

exciting _____

fun _____

fishing _____

flying drones _____

flying kites _____

listening to music _____

playing computer games

_____

riding a bike _____

singing songs _____

taking pictures _____

watching movies _____

Unit 3 Let's Go Shopping Tomorrow

afternoon _____

go camping _____

go hiking _____

go in-line skating _____

go jogging _____

go shopping _____

go skating _____

go skiing _____

go swimming _____

morning _____

today _____

tomorrow _____

weekend _____

Unit 4 What Do You Do After School?

clean my room _____

do my homework _____

have a piano lesson _____

help my mom _____

make a robot _____

play tennis _____

play with friends _____

read books _____

take a robot class _____

take an English class _____

watch music videos _____

walk my dog _____

wash her hands _____

Unit 5 — What Time Do You Get Up?

early _____
every day _____
exercise _____
get up _____
go home _____
go to bed _____
go to school _____
have breakfast _____
have dinner _____
have lunch _____
late _____
study English _____
together _____

Unit 6 — I Have Some Snacks in My Bag

blanket _____
camera _____
comic book _____
flashlight _____
lunchbox _____
map _____
picture _____
pot _____
sleeping bag _____
snack _____
tent _____
toy box _____
water bottle _____

Unit 7 — Whose Ball Is This?

balloon _____
cell phone _____
dress _____
hairpin _____
helmet _____
mirror _____
paintbrush _____
painting _____
shoes _____
textbook _____
toothbrush _____
wallet _____
watch _____

Unit 8 — Where Is the Bookstore?

bakery _____
behind _____
between _____
bookstore _____
bus stop _____
in front of _____
museum _____
next to _____
police station _____
post office _____
restaurant _____
train station _____
zoo _____

Syllabus 4A

Unit 1 Where Are You From?

Structures	Vocabulary		Grammar
• Where are you from?	Australia	Korea	my, your, his, her
I'm from France.	Canada	Mexico	
• Where is he from?	China	the U.S.	
He's from Korea.	France	Vietnam	
• Her name is Emma.			Reading

Unit 2 Do You Like Watching Movies?

Structures	Vocabulary		Grammar
• Do you like watching movies?	fishing	riding a bike	like playing
Yes, I do. / No, I don't.	flying drones	taking pictures	
• It looks fun.	listening to music	watching movies	
	playing computer games	singing songs	
			Reading

Review 1

Unit 3 Let's Go Shopping Tomorrow

Structures	Vocabulary		Grammar
• Let's go shopping tomorrow.	go camping	go shopping	go skating
Sounds good.	go hiking	go skating	
Sorry, I can't. I'm busy.	go in-line skating	go skiing	
• I need new socks.	go jogging	go swimming	
• How about tomorrow?			Reading

Unit 4 What Do You Do After School?

Structures	Vocabulary		Grammar
• What do you do after school?	do my homework	play with friends	-s, -es
I ride my bike.	have a piano lesson	take a robot class	
• What about you?	help my mom	take an English class	
• Sounds fun/good/great.	play tennis	walk my dog	
			Reading

Review 2

Unit 5 What Time Do You Get Up?

Structures	Vocabulary		Grammar

• What time do you get up?
  I get up at 6:30.
• Do you exercise every day?
  Yes, I do.
	exercise
	get up
	go home
	go to bed
		go to school
		have breakfast
		have dinner
		have lunch
			-es, -ies, has

			Reading

Unit 6 I Have Some Snacks in My Bag

Structures	Vocabulary		Grammar
• What do you have? I have some snacks. • What does she have? She has a blanket. • Do you have a blanket? Yes, I do. / No, I don't. • I have a camera in my bag.	blanket camera flashlight lunchbox	map pot sleeping bag water bottle	has, doesn't have
			Reading
Review 3			

Unit 7 Whose Ball Is This?

Structures	Vocabulary			Grammar

• Is this your ball?
  Yes, it is. It's mine.
  No, it isn't. It's not mine.
• Whose ball is this?
  It's Bob's.
	balloon
	bike
	cell phone
	dress
	hairpin
		helmet
		mirror
		paintbrush
		painting
		scarf
			textbook
			toothbrush
			umbrella
			wallet
			watch
				mine, yours, hers, his

				Reading

Unit 8 Where Is the Bookstore?

Structures	Vocabulary			Grammar

• Excuse me.
• Where is the bookstore?
  It's next to the toy shop.
  It's over there.
• Thank you.
  You're welcome.
	behind
	between
	in front of
	next to
		bakery
		bookstore
		bus stop
		museum
		police station
			post office
			restaurant
			toy shop
			train station
			zoo
				in front of, next to,
				behind, between

				Reading
Review 4				

Midterm TEST 4A

Institute _____

Name _____

Score ___/100

[1-2] Listen and choose.
잘 듣고, 알맞은 그림을 고르세요.

1
ⓐ
ⓑ
ⓒ
ⓓ

2
ⓐ
ⓑ
ⓒ
ⓓ

3 Listen and choose.
잘 듣고, 내용과 일치하지 않는 것을 고르세요.

ⓐ
ⓑ
ⓒ
ⓓ

[4-5] Listen and mark ○ or ✕.
잘 듣고 그림에 알맞으면 ○ 표, 그렇지 않으면 ✕ 표 하세요.

4
( )

5
( )

[6-7] Listen and choose.
잘 듣고, 대화의 빈칸에 알맞은 것을 고르세요.

6
A: _____

B: He's from China.

ⓐ   ⓑ   ⓒ   ⓓ

7
A: _____

B: No, I don't.

ⓐ   ⓑ   ⓒ   ⓓ

8 Listen and choose.
잘 듣고, 성격이 다른 것을 고르세요.

ⓐ   ⓑ   ⓒ   ⓓ

9 Listen and choose.
잘 듣고, 알맞은 것을 고르세요.

ⓐ
ⓑ
ⓒ
ⓓ

10 Listen and choose.
잘 듣고, 이어질 응답을 고르세요.

ⓐ   ⓑ   ⓒ   ⓓ

[11-12] Look and choose.
그림을 보고 여자아이가 할 말로 알맞은 것을 고르세요.

11

ⓐ Let's go camping.

ⓑ Let's go hiking.

ⓒ Let's go skiing.

ⓓ Let's go in-line skating.

12

ⓐ I'm from Vietnam.

ⓑ I'm from Canada.

ⓒ I'm from Mexico.

ⓓ I'm from China.

13 Read and choose.
다음을 읽고 알맞은 것을 고르세요.

I do my homework.

ⓐ    ⓑ

ⓒ    ⓓ

[14-15] Unscramble.
단어를 배열하여 문장을 완성하세요.

14

_____ after school?

(do / What / you / do)

15

_____?

(you / are / from / Where)

16 Read and choose.
다음을 읽고 어색한 것을 고르세요.

ⓐ My name is Ray.

ⓑ Tom likes riding a bike.

ⓒ She has a piano lesson.

ⓓ Let's go swim this afternoon.

[17-18] Read and choose.
대화를 읽고 빈칸에 알맞은 것을 고르세요.

17

A: Does he like taking pictures?

B: _____ He likes fishing.

ⓐ Yes, I do.

ⓑ Yes, he does.

ⓒ No, he doesn't.

ⓓ No, I'm not.

18

A: Let's go shopping.

B: _____ I'm busy.

ⓐ Okay.

ⓑ Sounds great.

ⓒ That's a good idea.

ⓓ Sorry, I can't.

[19-20] Look and write.
그림을 보고 빈칸에 알맞은 말을 쓰세요.

19

A: Do you like _____ _____?

B: Yes, _____ _____.

20

A: Where _____ _____ from?

B: He's _____ _____.

Final TEST 4A

Institute _____

Name _____

Score ___/100

[1-2] Listen and choose.
잘 듣고, 알맞은 것을 고르세요.

1 ⓐ   ⓑ

ⓒ   ⓓ

2 ⓐ  ⓑ

ⓒ  ⓓ

[3-4] Listen and choose.
잘 듣고, 그림에 알맞은 것을 고르세요.

3  ⓐ ⓑ ⓒ ⓓ

4  ⓐ ⓑ ⓒ ⓓ

5 Listen and choose.
잘 듣고, 주어진 질문에 알맞은 응답을 고르세요.

Whose mirror is this?

ⓐ   ⓑ   ⓒ   ⓓ

6 Listen and choose.
잘 듣고, 그림에 알맞은 응답을 고르세요.

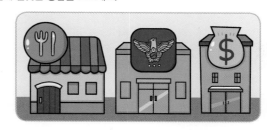

ⓐ   ⓑ   ⓒ   ⓓ

7 Listen and choose.
잘 듣고, 알맞은 그림을 고르세요.

ⓐ  ⓑ

ⓒ  ⓓ

[8-9] Listen and choose.
잘 듣고, 이어질 응답으로 알맞은 것을 고르세요.

8 ⓐ I have a flashlight.

ⓑ He has a flashlight.

ⓒ He has a sleeping bag.

ⓓ Yes, it's Bob's bag.

9 ⓐ It's Tina's.

ⓑ It's mine.

ⓒ It's a cell phone.

ⓓ I have a cell phone.

10 Listen and choose.
잘 듣고, 어색한 대화를 고르세요.

ⓐ   ⓑ   ⓒ   ⓓ

[11-12] Look and choose.
그림을 보고 알맞은 것을 고르세요.

11
ⓐ He has a map.
ⓑ He has a pot.
ⓒ He has a lunchbox.
ⓓ He has a helmet.

12
ⓐ It's Lucy's textbook.
ⓑ It's Lucy's wallet.
ⓒ It's Lucy's cell phone.
ⓓ It's Lucy's painting.

13 Read and choose.
다음을 읽고 그림에 알맞지 않은 것을 고르세요.

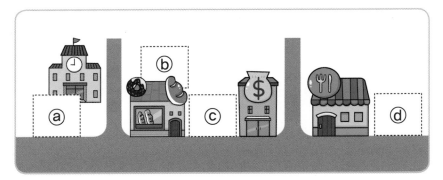

ⓐ It's in front of the school.
ⓑ It's in front of the bakery.
ⓒ It's between the bakery and the bank.
ⓓ It's next to the restaurant.

[14-15] Read and choose.
대화의 빈칸에 알맞은 것을 고르세요.

14
A: _____
B: It's mine.

ⓐ What's this?
ⓑ Is this your paintbrush?
ⓒ Whose mirror is that?
ⓓ Whose shoes are these?

15
A: What time do you have dinner?
B: _____

ⓐ It's 8 o'clock.
ⓑ Let's have dinner together.
ⓒ I have dinner at 7:30.
ⓓ That's very early.

16 Read and choose.
빈칸에 알맞은 것을 고르세요.

It's Mary's toothbrush. → It's _____.

ⓐ she   ⓑ hers   ⓒ her   ⓓ mine

17 Read and write.
빈칸에 공통으로 알맞은 말을 쓰세요.

· I have a tent _____ my bag.
· The bike is _____ front of the tree.

18 Unscramble.
단어를 배열하여 문장을 쓰세요.

_____?
(it / blanket / is / Whose)

[19-20] Look and write.
그림을 보고 빈칸에 알맞은 말을 쓰세요.

19

A: What time _____ he _____?
B: He _____ _____ 3:30.

20

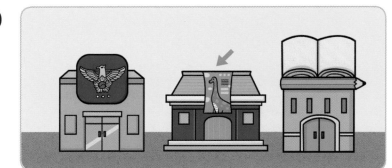

A: Where is the museum?
B: It's _____ the police station

and the _____.

2nd Edition

LET'S GO

to the English World

4A

2nd Edition

LET'S GO

to the English World

4A

Word Book
& Workbook

CHUNJAE EDUCATION, INC.

Word Book

Where Are You From?

A Listen and repeat. 🎧01 🎧02

France 프랑스	**I'm from France.** 나는 프랑스에서 왔어.
Korea 한국	**She's from Korea.** 그녀는 한국에서 왔어.
Canada 캐나다	**He's from Canada.** 그는 캐나다에서 왔어.
China 중국	**We're from China.** 우리는 중국에서 왔어.
the U.S. 미국	**Are you from the U.S.?** 너는 미국에서 왔니?
Vietnam 베트남	**Are they from Vietnam?** 그들은 베트남에서 왔니?
Australia 호주	**Is she from Australia?** 그녀는 호주에서 왔니?
Mexico 멕시코	**Is he from Mexico?** 그는 멕시코에서 왔니?

B Read, write, and say.

☐ Read ☐ Write ☐ Say

1 France
프랑스

_____ _____ _____

2 Korea
한국

_____ _____ _____

3 Canada
캐나다

_____ _____ _____

4 China
중국

_____ _____ _____

5 the U.S.
미국

_____ _____ _____

6 Vietnam
베트남

_____ _____ _____

7 Australia
호주

_____ _____ _____

8 Mexico
멕시코

_____ _____ _____

Learn More

Who 누구	Who is that girl? 저 여자애는 누구니?
Where 어디에	Where are you from? 너는 어디에서 왔니?
Her 그녀의	Her name is Ling. 그녀의 이름은 링이야.
This is 이 사람은	This is my friend, Antonio. 이 애는 내 친구 안토니오야.

Unit 1 **3**

A **Listen and repeat.** 14 15

fishing 낚시하기	**Do you like fishing?** 너는 낚시하는 것을 좋아하니?
flying drones 드론 날리기	**Does he like flying drones?** 그는 드론 날리는 것을 좋아하니?
watching movies 영화 보기	**Do they like watching movies?** 그들은 영화 보는 것을 좋아하니?
playing computer games 컴퓨터 게임 하기	**I like playing computer games.** 나는 컴퓨터 게임 하는 것을 좋아해.
taking pictures 사진 찍기	**Jane likes taking pictures.** 제인은 사진 찍는 것을 좋아해.
riding a bike 자전거 타기	**I don't like riding a bike.** 나는 자전거 타는 것을 좋아하지 않아.
listening to music 음악 듣기	**Dad doesn't like listening to music.** 아빠는 음악 듣는 것을 좋아하지 않으셔.

4

B Read, write, and say.

☐Read ☐Write ☐Say

1 fishing
낚시하기

_____ _____ _____

2 flying drones
드론 날리기

_____ _____ _____

3 watching movies
영화 보기

_____ _____ _____

4 playing computer games
컴퓨터 게임 하기

_____ _____ _____

5 taking pictures
사진 찍기

_____ _____ _____

6 riding a bike
자전거 타기

_____ _____ _____

7 listening to music
음악 듣기

_____ _____ _____

Learn More

fun 재미있는	**It looks** fun. 그것은 재미있어 보여.
exciting 신나는, 흥미진진한	**It's very** exciting. 그것은 아주 흥미진진해.
hip-hop music 힙합 음악	**I like** hip-hop music. 나는 힙합 음악을 좋아해.
singing songs 노래 부르기	**Do you like** singing songs? 너는 노래 부르는 것을 좋아하니?

A Listen and repeat. 🎧27 🎧28

go camping 캠핑하러 가다	**Let's** go camping. 캠핑하러 가자.
go hiking 하이킹하러 가다	**Let's** go hiking **tomorrow.** 내일 하이킹하러 가자.
go skiing 스키 타러 가다	**Let's** go skiing **tomorrow.** 내일 스키 타러 가자.
go skating 스케이트 타러 가다	**Let's** go skating **this afternoon.** 오늘 오후에 스케이트 타러 가자.
go jogging 조깅하러 가다	**Let's** go jogging **this evening.** 오늘 저녁에 조깅하러 가자.
go in-line skating 인라인스케이트 타러 가다	**Let's** go in-line skating **today.** 오늘 인라인스케이트 타러 가자.
go swimming 수영하러 가다	**Let's** go swimming **today.** 오늘 수영하러 가자.
go shopping 쇼핑하러 가다	**Let's** go shopping **now.** 지금 쇼핑하러 가자.

B Read, write, and say.

1 go camping
캠핑하러 가다

_____ _____ _____

2 go hiking
하이킹하러 가다

_____ _____ _____

3 go skiing
스키 타러 가다

_____ _____ _____

4 go skating
스케이트 타러 가다

_____ _____ _____

5 go jogging
조깅하러 가다

_____ _____ _____

6 go in-line skating
인라인스케이트 타러 가다

_____ _____ _____

7 go swimming
수영하러 가다

_____ _____ _____

8 go shopping
쇼핑하러 가다

_____ _____ _____

Learn More

today 오늘	Let's fly drones today. 오늘 드론을 날리자.
tomorrow 내일	Let's watch a movie tomorrow. 내일 영화를 보자.
this afternoon 오늘 오후	Let's take pictures this afternoon. 오늘 오후에 사진을 찍자.

What Do You Do After School?

A Listen and repeat.

play tennis 테니스를 치다	**We** play tennis **after school.** 우리는 방과 후에 테니스를 쳐.
play with friends 친구들과 놀다	**He** plays with friends **after lunch.** 그는 점심 식사 후에 친구들과 놀아.
help my mom 엄마를 돕다	**I** help my mom **after dinner.** 나는 저녁 식사 후에 엄마를 도와.
walk my dog 내 개를 산책시키다	**I** walk my dog **after school.** 나는 방과 후에 내 개를 산책시켜.
do my homework 숙제를 하다	**I** do my homework **after dinner.** 나는 저녁 식사 후에 숙제를 해.
take an English class 영어 수업을 듣다	**She** takes an English class **after school.** 그녀는 방과 후에 영어 수업을 들어.
take a robot class 로봇 수업을 듣다	**Do you** take a robot class **after school?** 너는 방과 후에 로봇 수업을 듣니?
have a piano lesson 피아노 레슨이 있다	**Do you** have a piano lesson **today?** 너는 오늘 피아노 레슨이 있니?

1 play tennis
테니스를 치다

_____   _____   _____

2 play with friends
친구들과 놀다

_____   _____   _____

3 help my mom
엄마를 돕다

_____   _____   _____

4 walk my dog
내 개를 산책시키다

_____   _____   _____

5 do my homework
숙제를 하다

_____   _____   _____

6 take an English class
영어 수업을 듣다

_____   _____   _____

7 take a robot class
로봇 수업을 듣다

_____   _____   _____

8 have a piano lesson
피아노 레슨이 있다

_____   _____   _____

Learn More

after school 방과 후에   **play soccer** 축구를 하다

after lunch 점심 식사 후에   **make a robot** 로봇을 만들다

after dinner 저녁 식사 후에   **read books** 책을 읽다

on Mondays 월요일마다   **watch music videos** 뮤직 비디오를 보다

Ⓐ **Listen and repeat.** 🎧53 🎧54

get up 일어나다	**What time do you** get up**?** 너는 몇 시에 일어나니?
have breakfast 아침을 먹다	**What time do you** have breakfast**?** 너는 몇 시에 아침을 먹니?
go to school 학교에 가다	**What time do you** go to school**?** 너는 몇 시에 학교에 가니?
have lunch 점심을 먹다	**I** have lunch **at 12:30.** 나는 12시 30분에 점심을 먹어.
go home 집에 가다	**He** goes home **at 4:40.** 그는 4시 40분에 집에 가.
exercise 운동하다	**Kelly** exercise**s at 6:20.** 켈리는 6시 20분에 운동해.
have dinner 저녁을 먹다	**Do you** have dinner **at 7?** 너는 7시에 저녁을 먹니?
go to bed 자다/자러 가다	**Do you** go to bed **at 11?** 너는 11시에 자니?

B Read, write, and say.

☐ Read ☐ Write ☐ Say

1 get up
일어나다

2 have breakfast
아침을 먹다

3 go to school
학교에 가다

4 have lunch
점심을 먹다

5 go home
집에 가다

6 exercise
운동하다

7 have dinner
저녁을 먹다

8 go to bed
자다/자러 가다

Learn More

early 이른(↔**late** 늦은)	**That's** very early. 그건 너무 일러.
every morning 매일 아침	**I go jogging** every morning. 나는 매일 아침 조깅하러 가.

one ten	**one twenty**	**one thirty**	**one forty**	**one fifty**
1시 10분	1시 20분	1시 30분	1시 40분	1시 50분

Unit 5 **11**

I Have Some Snacks in My Bag

A Listen and repeat. 🎧66 🎧67

blanket 담요	**I have a blanket.** 나는 담요를 가지고 있어.
map 지도	**Dad has a map.** 아빠는 지도를 가지고 계셔.
water bottle 물병	**Eva has a water bottle.** 에바는 물병을 가지고 있어.
pot 냄비	**I don't have a pot.** 나는 냄비를 가지고 있지 않아.
camera 카메라	**I have a camera in my bag.** 나는 가방에 카메라를 가지고 있어.
flashlight 손전등	**I have a flashlight in my bag.** 나는 가방에 손전등을 가지고 있어.
lunchbox 점심 도시락	**Do you have a lunchbox in your bag?** 너는 가방에 점심 도시락을 가지고 있니?
sleeping bag 침낭	**Does she have a sleeping bag?** 그녀는 침낭을 가지고 있니?

B **Read, write, and say.**

☐ Read ☐ Write ☐ Say

1 blanket
담요

_____ _____ _____

2 map
지도

_____ _____ _____

3 water bottle
물병

_____ _____ _____

4 pot
냄비

_____ _____ _____

5 camera
카메라

_____ _____ _____

6 flashlight
손전등

_____ _____ _____

7 lunchbox
점심 도시락

_____ _____ _____

8 sleeping bag
침낭

_____ _____ _____

Learn More

snack 간식	I have some snacks. 나는 약간의 간식을 가지고 있어.
comic book 만화책	I have comic books, too. 나는 만화책도 가지고 있어.
many things 많은 물건들	I have many things in my box. 나는 상자에 많은 물건들을 가지고 있어.

Whose Ball Is This?

Ⓐ Listen and repeat. 🎧79 🎧80

mirror 거울	**Whose mirror is this?** 이것은 누구의 거울이니?
paintbrush 그림 붓	**Whose paintbrush is this?** 이것은 누구의 그림 붓이니?
cell phone 휴대 전화	**Whose cell phone is that?** 저것은 누구의 휴대 전화니?
painting 그림	**Is this your painting?** 이것은 너의 그림이니?
toothbrush 칫솔	**Is this your toothbrush?** 이것은 너의 칫솔이니?
wallet 지갑	**It's my wallet.** 그것은 내 지갑이야.
textbook 교과서	**It's Sam's textbook.** 그것은 샘의 교과서야.
helmet 헬멧	**They're my brother's helmets.** 그것들은 내 형의 헬멧이야.

B Read, write, and say.

1 mirror
거울
_____ _____ _____

2 paintbrush
그림 붓
_____ _____ _____

3 cell phone
휴대 전화
_____ _____ _____

4 painting
그림
_____ _____ _____

5 toothbrush
칫솔
_____ _____ _____

6 wallet
지갑
_____ _____ _____

7 textbook
교과서
_____ _____ _____

8 helmet
헬멧
_____ _____ _____

Learn More

Whose 누구의   Whose **ball is this?** 이것은 누구의 공이니?

mine 나의 것   It's **mine.** 그것은 나의 것이야.

yours 너의 것   Is this **yours?** 이것은 너의 것이니?

lady bug 무당벌레   **watch** 손목시계   **balloon** 풍선   **hairpin** 머리핀

Ⓐ Listen and repeat. 🎧92 🎧93

in front of ~ 앞에	**The bus stop is in front of the hospital.** 버스 정류장은 병원 앞에 있어.
next to ~ 옆에	**The train station is next to the zoo.** 기차역은 동물원 옆에 있어.
behind ~ 뒤에	**The post office is behind the museum.** 우체국은 박물관 뒤에 있어.
between ~ 사이에	**It's between the bank and the bakery.** 그것은 은행과 빵집 사이에 있어.
train station 기차역	**Where is the train station?** 기차역은 어디에 있나요?
restaurant 식당	**Where is the restaurant?** 식당은 어디에 있나요?
post office 우체국	**It's behind the post office.** 그것은 우체국 뒤에 있어.
bus stop 버스 정류장	**The bus stop is over there.** 버스 정류장은 저쪽에 있어.

B Read, write, and say.

1 in front of
~ 앞에

_____ _____ _____

2 next to
~ 옆에

_____ _____ _____

3 behind
~ 뒤에

_____ _____ _____

4 between
~ 사이에

_____ _____ _____

5 train station
기차역

_____ _____ _____

6 restaurant
식당

_____ _____ _____

7 post office
우체국

_____ _____ _____

8 bus stop
버스 정류장

_____ _____ _____

Learn More

zoo 동물원	**bank** 은행	**hospital** 병원
park 공원	**police station** 경찰서	**town** 마을, 동네
museum 박물관	**bakery** 빵집	**ice cream shop** 아이스크림 가게
bookstore 서점	**school** 학교	**library** 도서관
toy shop 장난감 가게	**supermarket** 슈퍼마켓	**mall** 쇼핑 몰

Workbook

Where Are You From?

Words

Ⓐ **Look and write the letter.**

ⓐ Canada	ⓑ Vietnam	ⓒ the U.S.
ⓓ Australia	ⓔ France	ⓕ Mexico

1

2

3

4

5

6

Ⓑ **Circle and write.**

1

I'm from _____.

(Korea / Vietnam)

2

Judy is from _____.

(France / Australia)

3

Chen is from _____.

(Mexico / China)

Practice

A Match and write.

1
> Hi, I'm Tom.
>
> I'm _____ _____

2
> Hi, my name is Lucy.
>
> I'm _____ _____.

3
> He's Long.
>
> He's _____ _____.

B Look and choose.

1

Where are you from?

ⓐ I'm from Vietnam.

ⓑ I'm from China.

2

Where are you from?

ⓐ I'm from Canada.

ⓑ I'm from France.

3

Where is she from?

ⓐ She's from Australia.

ⓑ She's from the U.S.

4

Where is he from?

ⓐ He's from Mexico.

ⓑ He's from Korea.

Write & Talk

Ⓐ Read and match.

1

A: Where are you from?

B: I'm from Canada.

ⓐ

2

A: Are you from Korea?

B: No, I'm not.

I'm from Vietnam.

ⓑ

3

A: Who is he?

B: He's my friend, Dan.

He's from Australia.

ⓒ

Ⓑ Look and write.

1

A: Where is Roy from?

B: He's _____ _____

2

A: _____ is she from?

B: She's _____ _____.

3

A: This is my friend, Chen.

B: _____ is he _____?

A: He's from _____.

Reading

Ⓐ Read and write.

> Hi, my name is Minji.
>
> I'm from Korea.
>
> I'm ten years old.
>
> I like *bulgogi* and *tteokbokki*!

1 What is the girl's name? ⋯▸ Her name is _____.

2 Where is she from? ⋯▸ She's from _____.

3 How old is she? ⋯▸ She's _____ _____ old.

4 What does she like? ⋯▸ She likes _____ and _____.

Ⓑ Look and write.

> 1. Name: Antonio
> 2. From: Mexico
> 3. Age: 11
> 4. Likes: tacos, burritos

1 His name is _____.

2 He's _____.

3 He's _____.

4 He likes _____.

Build Up

A Circle and rewrite.

1

Is this (you / your) teddy bear?

····▶ _____

2

(She / Her) name is Grace.

····▶ _____

3

Harry likes (his / her) dog.

····▶ _____

4

Where is (he / his) from?

····▶ _____

B Read and write.

my	your	Her	His

1 I have a cat. I love _____ cat.

2 This is my brother. _____ name is Mike.

3 Wash _____ hands, please.

4 She's from France. _____ name is Emma.

24

A Make the sentence.

1 _____

(from / I'm / Canada / .) 나는 캐나다에서 왔어.

2 _____

(from / Kate / the U.S. / is) 케이트(Kate)는 미국에서 왔어.

3 _____

(you / are / from / Where / ?) 너는 어디에서 왔니?

4 _____

(is / Where / from / he / ?) 그는 어디에서 왔니?

5 _____

(China / you / from / Are / ?) 너는 중국에서 왔니?

6 _____

(is / Her / Ling / name / .) 그녀의 이름은 링(Ling)이야.

7 _____

(my / This / friend. / is / Antonio / .) 이 아이는 나의 친구, 안토니오(Antonio)야.

Do You Like Watching Movies?

Words

A Look and match.

1

riding •   • movies

2

flying •   • a bike

3

watching •   • computer games

4

playing •   • drones

B Look and write.

fishing

taking pictures

listening to music

1

I like _____.

2

I like _____.

3

I like _____.

Practice

A Circle and write.

1

Do you like (taking pictures / watching movies)?

_____

2

Do you like (fishing / playing computer games)?

_____

3

Do you like (listening to music / riding a bike)?

_____

B Read and write the letter.

ⓐ 　　ⓑ 　　ⓒ 　　ⓓ

1
A: Do you like watching movies?
B: No, I don't.　☐

2
A: Do you like fishing?
B: Yes, I do.　☐

3
A: Do you like listening to music?
B: Yes, I do.　☐

4
A: Do you like flying drones?
B: No, I don't.　☐

Write & Talk

A Read and match.

1   Do you like taking pictures?   •

 ⓐ   •   Yes, I do.

2   Does she like fishing?   •

 ⓑ   •   No, he doesn't.

3   Does he like singing songs?   •

 ⓒ   •   Yes, she does.

| watching movies | listening to music |
| riding a bike | playing computer games |

B Write and check.

1

Do you like _____?

☐ Yes, I do. ☐ No, I don't.

2

Do you like _____?

☐ Yes, I do. ☐ No, I don't.

3

Does she like _____?

☐ Yes, she does. ☐ No, she doesn't.

4

Does he like _____?

☐ Yes, he does. ☐ No, he doesn't.

Reading

A Read and write.

 I like _____ drones.

It's very _____.

I fly my drone in the park.

Do you _____ flying drones?

No, I don't.

I _____ fly drones.

I like _____ to music.

I like hip-hop music.

| can't | like | listening | flying | exciting |

B Look and write.

1

A: Do you like _____?

B: Yes, _____.

2

A: Does he like _____?

B: _____, he _____.

3

A: Does she like _____?

B: _____

4

A: Do you like flying kites?

B: No, _____. I like _____.

Build Up

(A) Read and circle.

1 I like (play / playing) baseball.

2 My sister likes (listening / listen) to music.

3 They like (dance / dancing) at the party.

4 Fred likes (take / taking) pictures.

5 We like (sing / singing) songs.

(B) Choose, correct, and write.

ride	watch	dance	fly

1

I like _____ a bike.

2

She likes _____ .

3

He likes _____ movies.

4

We like _____ kites.

Ⓐ Make the sentence.

1 _____

(taking / pictures / I / like / .) 나는 사진 찍는 것을 좋아해.

2 _____

(flying / likes / drones / He / .) 그는 드론 날리는 것을 좋아해.

3 _____

(playing / She / computer games / likes / .) 그녀는 컴퓨터 게임 하는 것을 좋아해.

4 _____

(you / Do / like / movies / watching / ?) 너는 영화 보는 것을 좋아하니?

5 _____

(like / Do / fishing / you / ?) 너는 낚시하는 것을 좋아하니?

6 _____

(music / Does / like / she / listening to / ?) 그녀는 음악 듣는 것을 좋아하니?

7 _____

(like / he / riding / Does / a bike / ?) 그는 자전거 타는 것을 좋아하니?

Let's Go Shopping Tomorrow

Words

Ⓐ Look and circle.

1

| go hiking | go swimming |

2

| go jogging | go in-line skating |

3

| go skating | go skiing |

4

| go shopping | go camping |

Ⓑ Read and write T or F.

1

Let's go shopping. ☐

2

Let's go skiing. ☐

3

Let's go swimming. ☐

4

Let's go in-line skating. ☐

Practice

(A) Look and write.

| go shopping | go swimming | go in-line skating | go hiking |

1
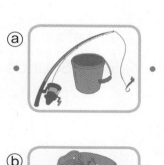
Let's _____.

2
Let's _____.

3

Let's _____.

4
Let's _____.

(B) Read and match.

1
A: Let's go camping.
B: Sorry, I can't.

ⓐ

2
A: Let's go jogging.
B: Sounds good.

ⓑ

3
A: Let's go fishing.
B: Sorry, I can't. I'm busy.

ⓒ

Write & Talk

A Read and write the letter.

ⓐ  ⓑ  ⓒ  ⓓ

1

A: Let's go in-line skating.

B: Sounds good. ☐

2

A: Let's go skating tomorrow.

B: Sounds great. ☐

3

A: Let's go swimming today.

B: Sorry, I can't.

I have a piano class. ☐

4

A: Let's go skiing this afternoon.

B: Sorry, I can't.

How about tomorrow?

A: Okay. ☐

B Write and choose.

1

A: Let's _____ this afternoon.

B: ⓐ Sounds great. ⓑ Sorry, I can't. I'm busy.

2

A: Let's _____ today.

B: ⓐ Okay. ⓑ Sorry, I can't. I'm tired.

3

A: Let's _____ tomorrow.

B: ⓐ Sounds good. ⓑ Sorry, I can't.

Reading

Ⓐ Read and number in order.

| 1 | Let's go camping tomorrow. |

| | I have a spoon and a fork. |

| 3 | Do you have a tent? |

| | Yes, I do. I have camping chairs, too. What do you have? |

| | That's a good idea. I like camping. I like eating steak, too. |

Ⓑ Look and write.

1

A: Let's _____ this weekend.

B: _____ good.

2

A: Let's _____ tomorrow.

B: _____ I'm busy.

tomorrow

this weekend

3

A: Let's _____ today.

B: That's a good _____.

this afternoon

today

4

A: Let's _____ this afternoon.

B: _____ I'm tired.

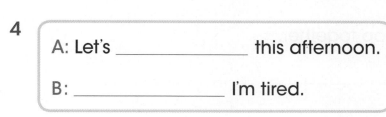

Build Up

Ⓐ Correct and rewrite.

1

Let's go <u>jog</u> this evening.

···▶ _____

2

Let's go <u>skate</u> tomorrow.

···▶ _____

3

Let's go <u>camp</u> this Saturday.

···▶ _____

4

Let's go <u>ski</u> this weekend.

···▶ _____

5

Let's go <u>swim</u> this afternoon.

···▶ _____

6

Let's go <u>shop</u> together.

···▶ _____

Writing

Ⓐ Make the sentence.

1 _____

(swimming / Let's / tomorrow / go / .) 내일 수영하러 가자.

2 _____

(go / this afternoon / Let's / shopping / .) 오늘 오후에 쇼핑하러 가자.

3 _____

(Let's / camping / this weekend / go / .) 이번 주말에 캠핑하러 가자.

4 _____

(hiking / Let's / today / go / .) 오늘 하이킹하러 가자.

5 _____

(a / idea / That's / good / .) 좋은 생각이야.

6 _____

(about / tomorrow / How / ?) 내일은 어때?

7 _____

(How / this weekend / about / ?) 이번 주말은 어때?

What Do You Do After School?

Words

A Look and write the letter.

> ⓐ play with friends ⓑ have a piano lesson ⓒ take a robot class
>
> ⓓ walk my dog ⓔ do my homework ⓕ play tennis

1

2

3

4

5

6

B Check and write.

1

	help my mom
	walk my dog

I _____ after school.

2

	play with friends
	take an English class

I _____ after school.

Practice

Ⓐ Look and match.

1

2

3

ⓐ I take a robot class after school.

ⓑ I help my dad after school.

ⓒ I play tennis after school.

Ⓑ Look and choose.

1

What do you do after school?

ⓐ I do my homework.

ⓑ I help my mom.

2

What do you do after school?

ⓐ I take a robot class.

ⓑ I take an English class.

3

What do you do after school?

ⓐ I have a piano lesson.

ⓑ I play with friends.

4

What do you do after school?

ⓐ I play tennis.

ⓑ I walk my dog.

Write & Talk

A Read and write.

helps her dad	takes a robot class	reads books
	have a piano lesson	watch TV

1

A: What do you do after lunch?

B: I _____.

2

A: What do you do after dinner?

B: I _____.

3

A: What does she do after school?

B: She _____.

4

A: What does he do after school?

B: He _____.

5

A: What does she do on Mondays?

B: She _____.

Reading

A Read, choose, and write.

A: What do you do after school, David?

B: 1 _____

A: Do you watch music videos, too?

B: 2 _____

A: What does Kate do after school?

B: 3 _____

A: Does Kate help her mom?

B: 4 _____

ⓐ Yes, I do.

ⓑ No, she doesn't.

ⓒ I take an English class.

ⓓ She plays with her dog.

B Read and match.

1
A: What do you do after school?
B: I help my mom.

•

ⓐ •

2
A: I do my homework after school.
  What about you?
B: I do my homework, too.

•

ⓑ •

3
A: Do you read books after school?
B: No, I don't. I walk my dog.

•

ⓒ •

Build Up

A Read and check.

| 1 | He play | |
| | He plays | |

| 2 | We read | |
| | We reads | |

| 3 | She watch | |
| | She watches | |

| 4 | Ann ride | |
| | Ann rides | |

| 5 | I take | |
| | I takes | |

| 6 | Tom walk | |
| | Tom walks | |

| 7 | I like | |
| | I likes | |

| 8 | He wash | |
| | He washes | |

| 9 | She listen | |
| | She listens | |

B Change and write.

1

She _____ to music. (listen)

2

He _____ soccer. (play)

3

My sister _____ a movie. (watch)

4

Mike _____ a bike. (ride)

A Make the sentence.

1 _____

(after school / have / I / a piano lesson / .) 나는 방과 후에 피아노 레슨이 있어.

2 _____

(walks / Kate / after school / her dog / .) 케이트(Kate)는 방과 후에 그녀의 개를 산책시켜.

3 _____

(soccer / I / with my friends / after lunch / play / .) 나는 점심 식사 후에 나의 친구들과 축구를 해.

4 _____

(They / TV / after dinner / watch / .) 그들은 저녁 식사 후에 텔레비전을 봐.

5 _____

(you / do / What / after school / do / ?) 너는 방과 후에 무엇을 하니?

6 _____

(What / he / do / does / after school / ?) 그는 방과 후에 무엇을 하니?

7 _____

(a robot class / Do / take / you / after school / ?) 너는 방과 후에 로봇 수업을 듣니?

What Time Do You Get Up?

Words

A Look and circle.

1

| get up | go to school |

2

| have lunch | have dinner |

3

| exercise | have breakfast |

4

| go to bed | go home |

B Look and write.

1

I _____ at 7:30.

2

I _____ at 8:00.

3

I _____ at 3:50.

4

I _____ at 12:30.

Practice

A Circle and write.

1

I (have breakfast / have lunch) at seven.

_____

2

I (go to school / go home) at eight thirty.

_____

3

I (get up / go to bed) at eleven ten.

_____

B Match and write the number.

1 What time do you get up? •

  • ⓐ I go home at 3:30.

2 What time do you exercise? •

  • ⓑ I exercise at 4:00.

3 What time do you have dinner? •

  • ⓒ I get up at 7:30.

4 What time do you go home? •

  • ⓓ I have dinner at 6:00.

Write & Talk

A Look and write.

thirty   twenty   forty   fifty   four   twelve

1

A: What time do you _____?

B: I go home at three _____.

2

A: _____ do you _____?

B: I have lunch at _____.

3

A: _____ do you _____?

B: I exercise at _____.

B Read, match, and write.

1
A: What time do you get up?

B: I _____ at _____.

2
A: What time do you have breakfast?

B: I _____ at _____.

3
A: What time do you go to bed?

B: I _____ at _____.

4
A: What time do you go to school?

B: I _____ at _____.

ⓐ

ⓑ

ⓒ

ⓓ

46

Reading

(A) Read, choose, and write.

A: 1 _____

B: He gets up at 7 o'clock.

A: Does he exercise there?

B: Yes. 2 _____

A: What does he do in the afternoon?

B: 3 _____

A: 4 _____

B: He goes to bed at 10 o'clock.

ⓐ What time does he go to bed?

ⓑ What time does Max get up?

ⓒ He listens to music.

ⓓ He rides a bike every day.

(B) Look and write.

1 	2 	3 	4 
8:00	8:30	4:20	5:50

1 What time do you _____? ····▸ I have breakfast at _____.

2 What time does he _____? ····▸ He goes to school _____.

3 What time do you _____? ····▸ I go home _____.

4 What time does she _____? ····▸ She has dinner _____.

Build Up

Ⓐ Change and write.

1 watch — watches

2 go — [　　　]

3 study — [　　　]

4 have — [　　　]

5 do — [　　　]

6 wash — [　　　]

Ⓑ Correct and rewrite.

1 He <u>go</u> swimming at two thirty.

...▸ _____

2 She <u>wash</u> her hair every morning.

...▸ _____

3 He <u>have</u> breakfast at seven.

...▸ _____

4 She <u>study</u> English after school.

...▸ _____

A Make the sentence.

1 _____

(do / get up / What time / you / ?) 너는 몇 시에 일어나니?

2 _____

(have dinner / you / do / What time / ?) 너는 몇 시에 저녁을 먹니?

3 _____

(at / go to school / eight twenty / I / .) 나는 8시20분에 학교에 가.

4 _____

(go home / I / five / at / .) 나는 5시에 집에 가.

5 _____

(twelve / She / at / has lunch / .) 그녀는 12시에 점심을 먹어.

6 _____

(goes / to bed / ten / He / at / .) 그는 10시에 자러 가.

7 _____

(every day / you / Do / exercise / ?) 너는 매일 운동하니?

UNIT 6 I Have Some Snacks in My Bag

Words

A Look and write.

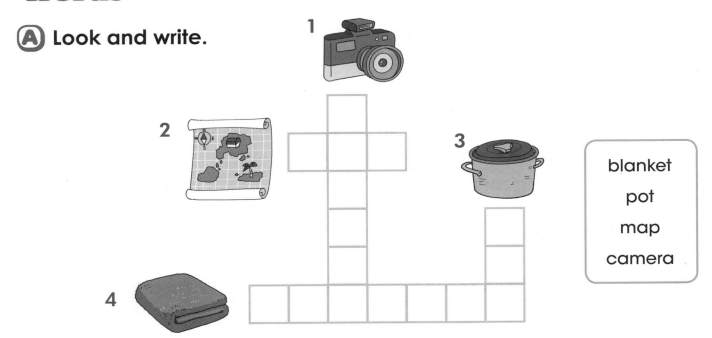

blanket
pot
map
camera

B Look and circle.

1    I have a (blanket / sleeping bag) in my bag.

2    I have a (water bottle / map) in my bag.

3    I have a (flashlight / camera) in my bag.

4    I have a (pot / lunchbox) in my bag.

Practice

A Read and write.

| blanket | sleeping bag | map | lunchbox |

1

A: What does he have?

B: He has a _____.

2

A: What does she have?

B: She has a _____.

3

A: What does James have?

B: He has a _____.

4

A: What does your sister have?

B: She has a _____.

B Read and match.

1 What does she have? •

2 What do you have? •

3 What does he have? •

• ⓐ He has a flashlight.

• ⓑ I have a water bottle.

• ⓒ She has a pot.

Write & Talk

A Look, match, and write.

1    2   3

1   What do you have?   •   • ⓐ   He has a _____ .

2   What does he have?   •   • ⓑ   I have a _____ .

3   Does she have a tent?   •

• ⓒ   No, she _____ .
She has a _____ .

B Read and number in order.

1   I'm thirsty. Do you have some water?

☐   Does she have a cup, too?

☐   No, I don't. Eva has a water bottle.

☐   Oh, good.

☐   I don't know.

5   Look. Kevin has a cup.

52

Reading

(A) Read and circle T or F.

I have many things in my box.

1 I have old books. (T / F)

2 I have a camera. (T / F)

3 I have a frog. (T / F)

Tom has many things in his box.

4 He has a robot. (T / F)

5 He has a kite. (T / F)

6 He has a map. (T / F)

(B) Read and write.

1

A: What do you have in your bag?

B: I _____.

2

A: What does she have in her bag?

B: She _____.

3

A: Does he have a sleeping bag?

B: _____, he doesn't.

He _____.

Build Up

A Read and circle.

1 I (**have** / has) a pencil case.

   I (**don't have** / doesn't have) a ruler.

2 Roy (have / **has**) a camera.

   He (don't have / **doesn't have**) a flashlight.

3 We (**have** / has) a tent.

   We (**don't have** / doesn't have) sleeping bags.

4 Tina (have / **has**) a lunchbox.

   She (don't have / **doesn't have**) a map.

B Look and write.

1

I _____ a sleeping bag.

I _____ a blanket.

2

Dennis _____ a map.

He _____ a flashlight.

3

He _____ a bike.

He _____ a car.

4

We _____ pots.

We _____ cameras.

Ⓐ Make the sentence.

1
_____

(What / you / do / have / ?) 너는 무엇을 가지고 있니?

2
_____

(you / in your bag / What / do / have / ?) 너는 가방에 무엇을 가지고 있니?

3
_____

(I / a map / in my bag / have / .) 나는 가방에 지도를 가지고 있어.

4
_____

(have / he / What / does / ?) 그는 무엇을 가지고 있니?

5
_____

(He / a water bottle / has / .) 그는 물병을 가지고 있어.

6
_____

(a tent / She / have / doesn't / .) 그녀는 텐트를 가지고 있지 않아.

7
_____

(a blanket / he / have / Does / ?) 그는 담요를 가지고 있니?

Whose Ball Is This?

Words

A Look and write the letter.

@ wallet	ⓑ mirror	© textbook
ⓓ helmet	ⓔ painting	ⓕ toothbrush

1

2

3

4

5

6

B Circle and write.

1

It's my _____.
(cell phone / wallet)

2

It's Kevin's _____.
(toothbrush / paintbrush)

3

It's Jane's _____.
(mirror / helmet)

Practice

A Read and write the letter.

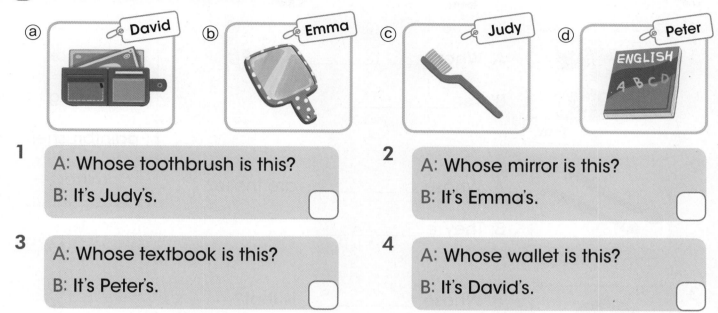

ⓐ David ⓑ Emma ⓒ Judy ⓓ Peter

1
A: Whose toothbrush is this?
B: It's Judy's. ☐

2
A: Whose mirror is this?
B: It's Emma's. ☐

3
A: Whose textbook is this?
B: It's Peter's. ☐

4
A: Whose wallet is this?
B: It's David's. ☐

B Circle and match.

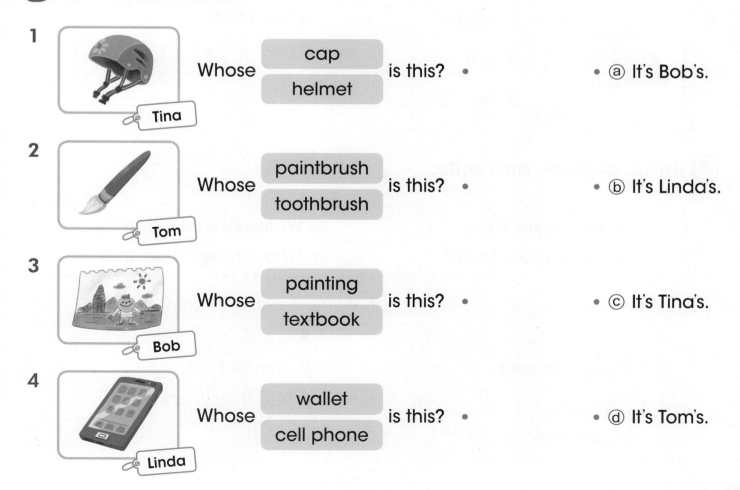

1 Tina
Whose [cap / helmet] is this? •   • ⓐ It's Bob's.

2 Tom
Whose [paintbrush / toothbrush] is this? •   • ⓑ It's Linda's.

3 Bob
Whose [painting / textbook] is this? •   • ⓒ It's Tina's.

4 Linda
Whose [wallet / cell phone] is this? •   • ⓓ It's Tom's.

Write & Talk

A Look and write.

1
Tony

A: Whose _____ is this?

B: It's _____ .

2
Paul

A: Whose _____ are these?

B: They're _____ .

3
Lisa

A: Whose _____ is that?
Is it Jane's?

B: No, it isn't. It's _____ .

4
Mike

A: Whose _____ is this, Mike?
Is it _____ ?

B: Yes, it's _____ .

| textbook |
| painting |
| paintbrushes |
| mirror |

B Read, choose, and write.

ⓐ No, they're Kate's.   ⓑ Whose helmet is this?

ⓒ Is this yours, Emily?   ⓓ Whose hairpins are these?

1

A: _____

B: It's Emily's helmet.

A: _____

C: Yes, it's mine.

2

A: _____

B: They're Eva's.

A: Are they yours, Eva?

C: _____

Reading

Ⓐ Read and match. Then write and color.

1

A: Whose dress is this?

B: It's _____ dress.
   She likes pink.

2

A: Whose hat is this?

B: It's _____ hat.
   She likes yellow.

3

A: Whose shoes are these?

B: They're _____.
   They're red and white.

ⓐ Name: Cindy

ⓑ Name: Dora

ⓒ Name: Anna

Ⓑ Look and write.

1

A: _____ is this?

B: It's _____ wallet.

2

A: _____ socks are these?

   Are these _____?

B: _____, they're not mine.

Build Up

A Read and circle.

1 This is (my / mine) bike. ⋯➤ It's (my / mine).

2 That is (her / hers) scarf. ⋯➤ It's (her / hers).

3 Is that (he / his) helmet? ⋯➤ Is that (he / his)?

4 Are they (your / yours) gloves? ⋯➤ Are they (your / yours)?

5 Are these (Jane / Jane's) shoes? ⋯➤ Are these (Jane / Jane's)?

B Correct and rewrite.

1 This is <u>yours</u> cell phone. ⋯➤ _____

2 The socks are <u>my</u>. ⋯➤ _____

3 Is this <u>your</u>, Mike? ⋯➤ _____

4 Tom's brother likes blue.

Is this <u>he's</u> wallet? ⋯➤ _____

5 A: Is this Jessica's dress?

B: No, it's not <u>her</u>. ⋯➤ _____

Writing

Ⓐ Make the sentence.

1 _____

(this / is / ball / Whose / ?) 이것은 누구의 공이니?

2 _____

(is / Whose / that / paintbrush / ?) 저것은 누구의 그림 붓이니?

3 _____

(shoes / these / Whose / are / ?) 이것들은 누구의 신발이니?

4 _____

(this / Is / textbook / your / ?) 이것은 너의 교과서니?

5 _____

(Anna / Is / yours. / that / ?) 저것은 너의 것이니, 안나(Anna)야?

6 _____

(helmet / Emily's / It's / .) 그것은 에밀리(Emily)의 헬멧이야.

7 _____

(not / it's / mine / No, / .) 아니, 그것은 내 것이 아니야.

Words

A Look and write the letter.

| ⓐ in front of | ⓑ between | ⓒ next to | ⓓ behind |

1

2

3

4

B Circle and write.

1

It's _____ the restaurant.

(next to / behind)

2

It's _____ the bakery and the post office.

(between / next to)

3

It's _____ the train station.

(in front of / behind)

4

It's _____ the hospital.

(between / in front of)

Practice

A Read and write T or F.

1

The bookstore is next to the restaurant. ☐

2

The library is behind the train station. ☐

3

The bank is between the post office and the hospital. ☐

B Read and match.

1
A: Where is the hospital?
B: It's behind the police station.

ⓐ

2
A: Where is the school?
B: It's in front of the park.

ⓑ

3
A: Where is the bakery?
B: It's next to the bookstore.

ⓒ

4
A: Where is the museum?
B: It's between the bank and the library.

ⓓ

Write & Talk

A Read and choose.

1

Where is the park?

ⓐ It's next to the train station.

ⓑ It's behind the museum.

2

Where is the bakery?

ⓐ It's next to the ice cream shop.

ⓑ It's between the bank and the restaurant.

3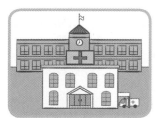

Where is the hospital?

ⓐ It's in front of the school.

ⓑ It's behind the police station.

B Match and write.

1

A: Where is the bus stop?

B: It's _____ the train station.

•   • ⓐ

2

A: Where is the bookstore?

B: It's _____ the restaurant _____ the toy shop.

•   • ⓑ

3

A: Where is the post office?

B: It's _____ the police station.

•   • ⓒ

Reading

A Read and write.

MY TOWN

This is my town.

My _____ is next to the police station.

The museum is _____ the park.

The post office is _____ the bank.

The _____ is between the library and the mall.

> in front of
>
> behind
>
> hospital
>
> school

B Look and write.

1 A: Where is the _____?

   B: It's _____.

2 A: Where is the _____?

   B: It's _____.

3 A: Where is the _____?

   B: It's _____.

Build Up

A Look and write.

1   The sofa is _____ the bookcase _____ the piano.

2   The table is _____ the sofa.

3   The sofa is _____ the table.

4   The piano is _____ the sofa.

5   The chair is _____ the piano.

6   The ball is _____ the doll _____ the robot.

7   The cat is _____ the box.

8   The bookcase is _____ the sofa.

A Make the sentence.

1 _____

(is / Where / the post office / ?) 우체국은 어디에 있나요?

2 _____

(the train station / is / Where / ?) 기차역은 어디에 있나요?

3 _____

(behind / It's / the museum / .) 그것은 박물관 뒤에 있어요.

4 _____

(It's / and / the restaurant / between / the bookstore / .) 그것은 서점과 식당 사이에 있어요.

5 _____

(is / the hospital / in front of / The bus stop / .) 버스 정류장은 병원 앞에 있어요.

6 _____

(next to / The school / is / the police station / .) 학교는 경찰서 옆에 있어요.

7 _____

(the library / between / is / and / the bank / The hospital / .) 병원은 도서관과 은행 사이에 있어요.